SAY 'NO' TO EXAM STRESS

Exams are important. The results can change lives and stressing about them can damage performance and undermine young peoples' confidence. This exam stress management programme requires very little time or effort to use and provides a straightforward, practical guide to exam stress management.

Written by an experienced educational psychologist, this short, explanatory book is accompanied by simple, easy to follow audio files which lead the listener through a sequence of five relaxation sessions to reduce stress, increase focus and plan for success. Using the book as a guide you simply listen to the audio tracks and follow what they say. All tracks have been designed so that they are easy to digest and applicable in the middle of a busy day. To sum up, this book:

- Provides practical and easy to follow steps to help anyone cope with exam stress
- Teaches relaxation techniques that can be used to reduce stress wherever you find it
- Offers a real stress knowledge base to teachers and family members supporting students with exam stress

This important guide is suitable for secondary school students as well as college and university students. The easy to follow relaxation sessions will be of interest to anyone studying for examinations who wishes to lower their exam stress levels.

Anthony James has a lifetime's experience working with children, parents, teachers and other professionals, as a chartered educational psychologist in both public and private sectors, ranging from rural communities to inner cities throughout the UK. He qualified as an educational psychologist at The University of Sussex, began working on stress management in the mid-1980s and subsequently completed a doctorate on teacher stress at University College London.

SAY 'NO' TO EXAM STRESS

The Easy to Use Programme to Survive Exam Nerves

Anthony James

Routledge
Taylor & Francis Group

LONDON AND NEW YORK

First published 2021
by Routledge
2 Park Square, Milton Park, Abingdon, Oxon OX14 4RN

and by Routledge
52 Vanderbilt Avenue, New York, NY 10017

Routledge is an imprint of the Taylor & Francis Group, an informa business

British Library Cataloguing-in-Publication Data
A catalogue record for this book is available from the British Library

Library of Congress Cataloging-in-Publication Data
Names: James, Anthony (Educational psychologist) author.
Title: Say 'no' to exam stress : the easy to use programme to survive exam
  nerves / Dr Anthony James.
Description: Abingdon, Oxon ; New York, NY : Routledge, 2020. | Includes
  bibliographical references and index. | Identifiers: LCCN 2020019458 |
  ISBN 9780367482558 (hardback) | ISBN 9780367482565 (paperback) |
  ISBN 9781003038863 (ebook)
Subjects: LCSH: Test anxiety. | Stress management. | Educational
  psychology.
Classification: LCC LB3060.6 .J36 2021 | DDC 371.2601/9–dc23
LC record available at https://lccn.loc.gov/2020019458

ISBN: 978-0-367-48255-8 (hbk)
ISBN: 978-0-367-48256-5 (pbk)
ISBN: 978-1-003-03886-3 (ebk)

Typeset in Joanna
by River Editorial Ltd, Devon, UK

Visit the eResources: www.routledge.com/9780367482565

CONTENTS

FOREWORD

Nowadays exam stress, sadly, is a reality for many students. This programme is a must for any young person who is looking for self-help techniques to deal with exam stress.

I have known the author since we started working together as educational psychologists in the mid-1990s. We developed stress management training, led by Tony, and spent several years providing courses for teachers and others in a local authority.

Over that lengthy period, as his co-presenter, I took part in his relaxation group sessions, relaxing alongside everyone else. I found these sessions very valuable, listening to his voice taking us through a stress management sequence.

Tony then completed a doctorate in stress management. Following that he published a detailed programme for teachers to use in providing their pupils with basic stress management skills.

Now you have the self-help students' programme which is the culmination of research, writing, trialling and refining over twenty-five years, all distilled into a straightforward, easily accessible book and recording. It is no mean feat to have made this information so user friendly, whilst staying true to the theory and research.

These stress management techniques are not to be learnt only from reading the written material. Students, benefit from listening to a recording of Tony's voice, relaxing, individually or in a group together, supporting each other in following and understanding the process. For life outside exams, these relaxation techniques can help people to deal with many other routine, stressful situations.

The book provides basic stress information for the time when you have a chance to read it. The underlying structure is soundly based on modern psychology, brought to you in an easy to use style, which can be summed up as 'choosing what to think'.

I can recommend this programme to any young person aiming to help themselves to deal positively with exam stress. Start up the recording and begin relaxing, but do also try to find time for the book, since there is a wealth of useful and easily accessible information here.

Dr Simon Claridge,
Consultant Psychologist and Honorary Tutor,
Cardiff University

INTRODUCTION

You have purchased a stress management programme which requires very little time or effort to use, has a base in well founded psychological principles, providing a straightforward, practical guide to stress management for students at college or school. In an easy to follow audio sequence, the young person is led through a series of five stress management sessions.

You start by reading Chapter 1, only a few pages, then listening to the first of the five recorded, relaxation scripts and follow what is said. Each recording lasts around 15–20 minutes. For busy people, Chapter 1 contains the programme condensed into one chapter. For those who can make time to look at background information and the psychology of stress, later chapters offer you additional detail. This can deepen your knowledge and provide you with material to share with your fellow students in gradual stages over time.

The last session, number 5 in the series, is the exam stress session but this is not a free standing session. You need to complete Sessions 1–4 before doing Session 5.

Chapter 1 is the complete programme in one chapter for people who would prefer to get started and read the detail later.

Chapter 2 provides more detail, if you feel you need it, on how to go through a stress management session.

Chapters 3 to 6 provide the basic information which is useful to know from the literature about stress and its management.

Chapter 7 tells you why it can be helpful for students to listen to the recording together in a small group of, say, two, three or four people.

Chapter 8 shows how straightforward it can be to fit stress management into your busy life.

Chapters 9 and 10 give the theoretical and philosophical bases for the programme.

1

A BRIEF OVERVIEW OF THE STRESS MANAGEMENT PROGRAMME

Read this chapter first

Too busy

You may be too busy to read all ten chapters in the programme and so the whole course has been concisely set out in this single chapter. This gives you all the basics. You can read other chapters at your leisure.

There are five audio relaxation sessions in this programme, and listening to each recording takes only 15–20 minutes. This may be helpful to students who are too busy studying to do much about managing the stress which often goes with studying and exams. Typically you would listen to one audio recording per week, although more often if you wish. It is important to listen to the audio recordings in order, 1–5.

Who is the programme for?

This programme is designed to help college and school students who are under stress from forthcoming exams. In practice, there is no upper age limit. In order to be effective, stress management techniques must be designed in a straightforward style; complexity can lead to stress. The same, simple programme suits a wide age range.

Underlying structure

This stress management programme is easy to follow, but there is some carefully structured thinking behind it. The principle is similar to the writing of a film or play. You may be watching a simple interaction of the characters but the script writers have created the plot, an underlying structure. This is designed to hold your attention by tapping into themes which interest you as a human being such as love, betrayal, rejection, triumph of the underdog and so on. The design of this stress management programme is similar, with a simple sequence of events on the surface and a psychological structure underneath to tackle the serious business of stress management.

Rationale of the programme

It seems unlikely that the purpose of life is to fill ourselves with stress. Stress management starts with sitting quietly and reflecting on the positive and satisfying aspects of life as a way of letting go our stressful thoughts. In quiet, reflective sessions, listening to the audio relaxation tracks, students are invited to look beyond themselves and see the pathway to a low stress life.

A small group of students relaxing together

When a small group of students listens together to a relaxation recording, this provides an opportunity for discussion afterwards about the calm feelings and pleasant thoughts which came to mind during the relaxation sequence. This discussion might occupy a few minutes immediately after the relaxation, or later the same day, during mealtime or instead of watching some of the usual evening's TV.

Sharing experiences of stress and its management with your fellow students can help release tension and act as an extra stress management technique.

Routine precautions

Do **not** listen to the recorded relaxation scripts while driving or controlling a vehicle.

Do **not** start or continue a relaxation session when to do so would distract you from, or be incompatible with, looking after yourself. For example, if you have left something on the stove you are free to set aside the relaxation session and deal with that (see Ending a session ahead of schedule, p 000).

Take care if you or anyone with you suffers from asthma, epilepsy or panic attacks, because relaxation can exacerbate or activate these conditions in rare cases (Palmer and Cooper, 2007).

The next section informs you in straightforward terms how to run through a relaxation session.

The basics of taking part in a relaxation session

Find a reasonably quiet place at home, or wherever you live. Sit or lie down, get as comfortable as possible, listen to the Track 1 relaxation recording and follow what it says. After the recording finishes you may like to sit quietly for a few moments and reflect on your thoughts during relaxation.

If your relaxation was in the company of a few other students you might share your experiences of relaxation. How easy was it to relax, what nice pictures you may have seen in your mind's eye and so on.

For the second and subsequent sessions, choose the time intervals which suit you. Session 2 could take place the following day or a week later. You repeat the process, listening to the Session 2 relaxation recording. Continue like that through to Session 5 (exam stress) to complete the sequence.

If you are part of a group of students and you feel in the mood, you could progress to a member of the group reading aloud one of the relaxation scripts (reprinted at the back of this book) instead of listening to the recording. This can increase the sense of the group working together to help each other in reducing stress.

After the five recorded relaxation sessions have been run through in order for the first time, in the weeks following, you may re-listen to some of the five recordings as a top up, in any order, from time to time as you wish.

Ending a session ahead of schedule

It may be that your phone rings, or someone knocks on your door and you have to leave the room to attend to something before the relaxation session is due to end. It is important to bring yourself out of the relaxation state before you start another task. You can do this by reading aloud to yourself the last paragraph from script for the relaxation recording: Track 1, which is:

> In a moment I am going to count out loud from 1–10.
> When I say the number 10, keeping hold of your calm feelings, open your eyes, be refreshed and feel alert as usual.
> 1-2-3-4-5-6-7-8-9-10.
> Open your eyes.
> You are now refreshed, fully alert and ready to do everything as usual.
> You are now refreshed, fully alert and ready to do everything as usual.

In fact it may be preferable if you turn off your phone or turn down the volume while you are relaxing and hang a 'Do not disturb' sign on the door. A session lasts only 15–20 minutes. It will probably be alright for you to be out of circulation for such a short time.

Choosing what to think

The five sessions are arranged in a sequence, with each session following a similar format which invites you to do two things: relax your muscles and 'choose what to think'. Choosing what to think means, for example, choosing to think about something positive and pleasant, say recalling a nice picture to your mind's eye, rather than thinking about something stressful.

In each successive audio recording there is repetition of wording from the previous script followed by some new wording. This repetition is intentional; it is important and it is not a 'filler'. Repetition gives you practice at muscle relaxation and choosing what to think. With practice you improve these stress management skills. In successive scripts the wording moves on from a pleasant picture in your mind's eye, to inviting you to think about a nice phrase or saying and so on. With each new wording the 'choosing what to think' changes to provide a developing stress management sequence.

The exam stress session

Stress management for exams requires a build up of stress management skills over a period of time before you learn the technique specific to exam stress. The audio track for Session 5 is the exam stress session, but this is not a free standing session. You need to do Sessions 1–4 before starting Session 5.

After you have built up your relaxation and choosing what to think skills over the four preceding sessions, the audio track for Session 5 guides you in how to use the 'touch on the wrist' as a relaxation prompt or reminder which can enable you to take your relaxation with you and feel relaxed anywhere, even travelling to an exam. The touch on the wrist technique is a portable stress reducer. You don't have to be in a quiet room, close your eyes or lie down to feel relaxed.

If you think that you might experience exam stress, you need to start getting practice on Session 1 when you start feeling worried. Doing one session per week you would take five weeks to get through this programme. Best to allow plenty of time and start on this programme, say, six to ten weeks or longer before the exams. If you are planning to take exams in the later stages of your school career and the school offers mock exams, that is a good opportunity to start practising your stress management skills in preparation for the mocks.

Preparation is the key

There is no avoiding the fact that good preparation and study, well in advance of the exams, may be the most effective way of reducing exam stress. If you are in the later stages of your school career, many schools have revision, exam technique and preparation guidelines which are important and can be used in conjunction with this programme.

As shown in Figure 1.1, students need to work sensibly and systematically from the start of each term.

The next step is to listen to the relaxation tracks 1–5 in the weeks or months running up to the exam. To remain calm travelling to, just before and during the exam, you can use the 'touch on the wrist' method of stress management which is taught to you in the Session 5 audio track.

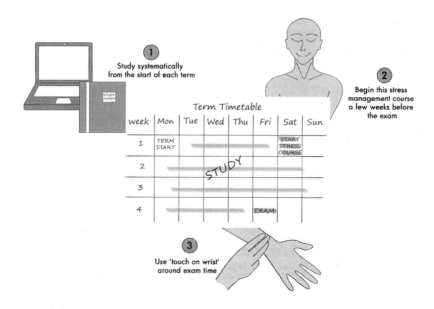

Figure 1.1 Three stages for dealing with exam stress

Why use 'touch on the wrist' for exam stress?

In Sessions 1–4 you listen to the audio Tracks 1–4 in numerical order, over a period of time, giving you practice at relaxation and choosing what to think. In Session 5, the audio track builds on your skills by adding the 'touch on the wrist' stress management technique. This is the exam stress management technique. The touch on the wrist is a portable stress management technique. It is a tangible reminder of your nice thoughts and feelings which you can take with you after the session is over.

When you have learnt this technique during an audio session, you simply touch yourself on the wrist anytime after the session is over and stress can be reduced in response to that touch. The difference from an audio relaxation session is that the touch on the wrist does not require you to find a quiet place or close your eyes.

This touch on the wrist technique is useful for exam stress because you can use it quickly, easily and without anyone noticing. You do not need to be seated, or lying down and it's portable. You can use it when walking, running, on the bus, during the exam – anywhere. You can use this quick stress management technique the night before the exam, the morning of the exam or travelling to the exam. Your stress will often reduce once the exam has started but if not, you can use the touch on the wrist during the exam.

Getting ready for exams: practical guidelines
In the months before the exam

- Listen to tips and hints for doing exams if your school or college provides these.
- Do your best in the booster classes if they are offered.
- Do your best in practice exams or tests if your school or college provides these.
- Revise, but plan a mixture of revision and 'down time'.
- Follow healthy eating guidelines which you learn about in school and elsewhere.

Just before the exam

If you are feeling a bit nervous the night before exams, try to find someone to talk to and use your touch on the wrist.

Make sure you do not go to bed late; go to bed at your usual time on the night before an exam.

Remember what you will need to take with you on exam day; get everything ready the night before.

As a final thought, 'preparation is the key'. If you know your stuff you are less likely to experience stress at the thought of being examined on it.

2

THE CONTENTS OF A STRESS MANAGEMENT SESSION

For students who would like more detail on taking part in a stress management session, this chapter spells it out.

Before the session

Decide the best time of the day for a session, within your daily routines. Times to avoid might be just before mealtimes when you might be distracted by hunger and just before you need to catch a bus.

Decide on a quiet room which you are going to use for your relaxation session. Decide which device you are going to use to play the audio track and have it ready. It may be best if you switch off your phone or put it on silent for the duration of the relaxation session. The room will need sufficient seating or space where you can sit or lie down in comfort.

Locate audio Track 1 on your device. (Track 1 is for Session 1, Track 2 for Session 2 and so on.)

Get comfortable seated or lying down.

If you are relaxing in a small group of students it is best if everybody avoids talking during a relaxation session. Talking disrupts concentration on the audio track.

If you need to stop the session part way through, for example, if you notice or remember something which needs your urgent attention, you will need to follow the instructions for Ending a Session Ahead of Schedule (p.000). Have a look at these instructions before the session starts. If you are one of a group and you need to stop, just leave the room and read the ending instructions quietly to yourself when you are outside the door.

In a group of students you might start things off by saying something like:

In a moment I am going to start playing a track from the relaxation audio.

There is no need to talk whilst the track is playing; in fact it is better not to talk as this will distract others.

The track lasts about fifteen minutes. All you have to do is listen, relax your muscles and so on, as suggested by the voice on the track.

Play the track.

Listen to the track and follow what it says.

After an audio track has finished

When Track 1 has finished, stop the audio playing.

If you have listened to the track as part of a small group of fellow students, you might invite each other to talk about how they felt and what they thought about the relaxation session, if they wish to do so. There may be no time for this discussion straight after the session, but you can talk later in the day or just before Session 2.

Each person might say something about their muscle relaxation, their thoughts and feelings. This may help to fix their good feelings in mind after the session is over. Sharing good feelings with each other may help to further reduce stress.

If you have listened to the track on your own there may be someone in your life who would be interested in hearing about your relaxation session. You might go through the discussion ideas below with a friend over lunch or in the bar that evening. Stress and its management is a topic which interests many people, even those who do not wish to actively tackle the issue.

Some ideas for discussion are suggested below.

- How relaxed were you? (More relaxed than a previous time?)
- What was your picture in your mind's eye?
- Was your picture in colour or black and white?
- Was your picture clear and sharp or slightly blurred?
- Was your picture moving or still like in a photograph?

These ideas for discussion can be used again at further sessions and some interesting changes might be noticed. For example, pictures might become clearer after repeated relaxation practice.

Session 2 onwards

You might listen to Track 1 on your first day with this programme, then Track 2 the following day or the following week and so on. Another approach might be to listen to Track 1 each day for one week, then listen to Track 2 each day for a second week and so on. You can decide which timing is best for you. At Session 2, repeat with Track 2 the process you followed with Track 1 and so on through to Track 5.

When you listen to the audio for the first time it is important to listen to Tracks 1–5 in order because each track builds on the track before it. Having completed the sequence of listening to Tracks 1–5 in order, after that you can pick any track you like and listen to the tracks in any order. After the basic training of Tracks 1–5 in order, say you decide to have a relaxation session once per week, just pick your favourite track and listen to it as a 'one off'. Say you pick Track 3, 'I breathe all my worries into a balloon'. You might like to listen to that track every week for a few weeks then change to Track 4, 'See yourself in your mind's eye helping a stressed person'. You might choose to listen to that for a week or two, then change again. The important thing is to keep in practice with your relaxation and choosing what to think skills.

In Track 1 for example, where you are invited to see a nice picture in your mind's eye, each person sees a different picture. The idea is that you will choose to see a picture which is of value to you. The same principle applies to the images suggested for each successive track. Your stress management training is thereby individualised.

3

LIFE CAN BE STRESSFUL

Let's start to unpack some of the causes of stress. With most people, stress seems to come from all around us. When stress arrives it can make you short tempered, argumentative and restless. Your stress can spread and affect the people around you.

Where does stress come from?

Stress can come from countless directions in everyday life. First let's look at some possible causes of stress for people everywhere, not only students.

- Chemicals – alcohol and drug abuse, food additives, etc.
- Children – offspring consistently make demands
- Communication – can be ambiguous and anxiety producing, even with our partner
- Commuting – usually contains traffic jams and similar frustrations
- Decision making – applying for courses or jobs, moving house, getting married at some stage

- Emotions – loss of self-esteem, taking things personally
- Finances – how will a mortgage be possible, stability of the financial system, credit card debts creeping up
- Health – such as poor sleeping, over or under eating, lack of exercise
- Life changes – such as having to live far from your family
- Life traumas – such as parental divorce, bereavement
- Marital problems – enough said!
- Physical challenges – from other motorists, fear of being mugged
- Phobias – many people have phobias, such as spiders, confined spaces
- Recreation – can be competitive, for example in sports and is therefore potentially stress inducing. Holidays can turn out disappointing and so we do not feel that our batteries have been re-charged
- Relationships – partner and flat sharing relationships
- Spiritual/psychological needs – may be pushed to one side in the rat race
- Time – there is never enough of it
- Work – there is always too much of it

In the future, after college, you may have stressors which are closely related to the workplace

- Organisational problems, for example you can be affected by unclear decision making processes
- Long or unsociable hours
- Poor status, pay and promotion prospects
- Unnecessary rituals to be completed on line
- Uncertainty and insecurity, such as frequent changes of policy
- Burn out or rust out culture of workplace
- Unclear role specifications
- Role conflict, where two aspects of a job are incompatible
- High expectations with too few resources
- Inability to influence decision making – a sense of powerlessness
- Not always appreciated by managers
- Isolation from support of colleagues
- Overwork, time pressures, lack of variety in the job
- Poor communication
- Conflicting and competing with colleagues

- Appraisals
- Insufficient training
- Constraints against actually getting the job done
- Manager behaviour

It may be possible to look at some of life's everyday events and give each a stress score.

Attempting to measure stress

There are many checklists which attempt to measure stress. One of the early attempts and maybe still one of the best known, is shown below. The idea is that you look at the list and note any items which have happened to you in the last 12 months (Holmes and Rahe, 1967).

A stress scale by Holmes and Rahe

Events	Stress weighting
Death of spouse	100
Divorce	73
Marital separation	65
Imprisonment	63
Death of close family member	63
Personal injury or illness	53
Marriage	50
Dismissal from work	47
Marital reconciliation	45
Retirement	45
Change in health of family member	44
Pregnancy	40
Sexual difficulties	39
Gaining new family member	39
Business readjustment	39
Change in financial state	38
Change in number of arguments with spouse	35
Major mortgage or loan	32
Foreclosure of mortgage or loan	30
Changes in responsibilities at work	29
Children leaving home	29
Trouble with in-laws	29
Outstanding personal achievement	28
Partner begins or stops work	28

(Continued)

Events	Stress weighting
Change in living conditions	28
Change in personal habits	26
Trouble with boss	25
Change in working hours or conditions	24
Change in residence	23
Change in schools or college	20
Change in recreation	20
Change in church activities	20
Change in social activities	19
Minor mortgage or loan	18
Change in sleeping habits	16
Change in number of family meetings	15
Change in eating habits	15
Holidays	13
Christmas	12
Minor violations of the law	11

Holmes and Rahe were doctors, psychiatrists who surveyed large numbers of medical patients to research this stress scale. They asked whether these patients had experienced any of the above events in the previous two years. They found this was the case and to get this feedback into perspective they scored each event with a different 'weight' for stress.

For our purposes, looking at the weighted scores above helps us to understand that everyday events such as holidays, can be stressful. It also helps to see that some events are more stressful than others. For example, divorce (given a high score of 73) is likely to be more stressful than taking out a loan (given a lower score of 18). Holmes and Rahe carried out various, fairly complicated calculations which showed that the higher a person's total score, the higher their likelihood of illness. It is generally accepted that stress can affect the immune system and so a link between stress and illness is not surprising.

However, you may not need a list of possible stress indicators. You possibly know what stresses you without being told. So what can we do about it? Let's start by looking at some simple ideas about stress management which people pick up from the media and from talking with friends.

4

GETTING TO GRIPS WITH STRESS

Reducing stress is easy?

As students it would seem likely that many of you have experienced stress, not only in relation to previous exams but in other aspects of life such as problems arising from your social life with others your own age and possibly your family life. In the world we live in, it is difficult to avoid stress arising from competition for attention and striving to be liked. You have probably found ways of tackling these stresses but you may have doubts about their effectiveness.

Relaxing with a drink may be one way of coping. In moderation this may be a helpful way of taking time out to think about what to do about stress. On the other hand, too much drink can lead to disturbed sleep, making us less able to cope with the following day's demands, and so we may end up more susceptible to stress. Over a period of time drink may lead to health problems, possibly adding further to your stress.

Some of us have hobbies and pursuits, such as reading, listening to music, sports and so on, which refresh and renew us. Nonetheless it can be difficult to maintain these interests under stress. Hobbies take time and thought, both of which can be in short supply when we are under stress. Do you know anybody who was an avid novel reader in their school days, who hasn't read a novel for years?

Physical exercise can be beneficial when a person is stressed. Exercise can leave you feeling more relaxed afterwards and promote better sleep. Energy to tackle potentially stressful events can be increased when we are more physically fit and eat healthily. Unfortunately taking exercise and planning a healthy diet can be forced off the agenda when we are under stress.

One of the principles behind this book is that, dealing with stress effectively requires a specific stress management technique. This programme aims to alleviate the mental and physical aspects of stress, without being too time consuming, expensive or impractical.

Simple hassle strategies for students: is this all you need?

Do we need to bother with an actual stress management programme which arises from a sound basis in the literature and follows a specified sequence of events? Why not just try a few simple strategies?

- Be aware of your body's reactions. Take a moment to think what is causing that churning in your stomach and perhaps you can do something about it.
- Don't take it personally when your tutor suggests that some changes must be made.
- Arrive at your lectures a bit earlier and you will be able to bag that parking space for your bike.
- Get together any books, papers and equipment for the next day and put them in your bag the night before. This avoids the stress of trying to find things in the morning just before you have to dash out of the door.
- Take three deep breaths and count to ten before you tell him or her how irritating they are. This hassle may sink without trace – you won't need to say anything in the end and there will be no fall out to deal with.
- Say to yourself, 'What I *actually* do today is all I *have* to do today.'[1]
- Remember a dignified and gracious person whom you know and imagine how he or she would react to the irritating situation you now find yourself in.

- Remember you are entitled to say, 'No', for example when someone invites you out for an evening's drinking, but it is best to do so in a matter-of-fact, assertive way rather than snappily or aggressively.
- Remind yourself of a little treat you have planned for yourself as a reward for your patience, tolerance, understanding and hard work.
- Set and follow your own clear priorities and realistic deadlines, with monitoring steps built in.
- Do not prevaricate – the fear of something going wrong is often worse than the actual action.
- Keep a real balance in life – exercise and relaxation enliven the body and mind.
- Ensure you take breaks. Slog away at one task and you can become less efficient.
- Have a laugh. Laughter releases endorphins which make you feel better.
- When you have done your work for the day, you have done your work.
- Take time to do something nice for someone every day and don't wait for recognition for it.
- Give and ask for honest feedback from your tutor on performance and what could have gone better.
- Remember you may need support – it's okay to ask.
- When you are going into a stressful situation take time to prepare and visualise how you will deal with it. If you recognise the difficulties and have a prepared strategy you won't get frozen into inactivity.
- After being in a stressful situation rehearse it: what went well, what went not so well, what could you have done differently. Turning something into a learning experience helps you see it from a different perspective and helps prepare you for the next time.

OK so far, but knowing about these techniques does not give you the motivation, the drive to put them into practice. You may know how to handle stress but stay stressed. We probably all know how to lose weight but that does not mean we go ahead and lose it. In order to manage our stress successfully we need a programme which we can buy into, which is meaningful to us and which engages us and motivates us.

Just another stress management programme?

This programme goes beyond simple hassle strategies. In designing this programme the author has tried to gather together, in a concise form, the work of several major psychologists and others who have thought carefully about people and how we get on with our lives. The writers and thinkers whose work has helped to form this programme are all named in the References section at the end and so you can look further should you wish to do so. The books and articles which these psychologists have written are often stuck on library shelves, gathering dust and not seen by the people who might find them beneficial. Unfortunately their work may be seen as rather academic and so it does not reach a wide audience.

So the author is not making up this programme as he goes along. Your life is too important to spend time reading one person's ideas on how to manage your stress. The author is a psychologist with a lifetime's experience of studying and applying the works of some major thinkers on the subject of human nature. The intention is to simplify their ideas and pass them on to you in a form which is easy to digest and apply in the middle of a busy day. If the structure and content of this programme is worthwhile it is because of the expertise of other writers and because the author has used and evaluated these methods over many years. This programme is not designed as 'flavour of the month'.

This programme is simple and quick to use, but it does not rely on techniques such as: prioritise your tasks for the day; make some time for yourself; give yourself treats; have a bubble bath and so on. There is merit in using these basic approaches, but this programme strives to go beyond the common sense of 'quick fix' and set out some distilled wisdom.

Let's start from a philosophical basis. Let's accept that life can be difficult and often presents to us a series of problems which can result in stress. It seems likely that there are many people who experience stress at some point or other in their lives. Getting a bit philosophical again, stress can make us feel that we are less than we are. We probably don't want that state of mind to continue. It seems unlikely that we want to sit there feeling stressed. We probably want to know how to live life to the full and ultimately teach our children how to do the same (Peck, 1978).

What this programme is not

We can explain something by saying what it is, but the explanation may become clearer when we say what it is not. This programme is not: take some exercise; walk away from the stressor; find an empty room and shout; count to ten; breathe deeply. Neither does this programme talk in broad terms such as: do not take on too much; find out what causes your stress; talk over your problem with somebody. This programme is not: take a relaxing bath at night; begin the day with a good breakfast and take a refreshing shower; have a massage to alleviate muscular tension; take your mind off things with a good novel; use cosmetics and products containing natural things such as lavender, to help reduce tension; take a 'power nap' in the middle of the day; visit a spa and get in touch with natural surroundings; smile – this will transmit a message to your brain that everything is OK; follow a balanced diet with a range of natural nutrients including fruits, vegetables, whole grains and fish. You may find some of these ideas to be helpful and they may get you started on stress management but this programme attempts to go a bit deeper.

There is plenty of advice available from other authors on the relationship between stress and healthy lifestyle factors such as diet, exercise, alcohol, caffeine intake and so on. You may find it valuable to consider some of their recommendations. However, this programme is based on psychology and how to apply it easily and fluently to an everyday, stressful life.

Note

1   Heard on a course at Landmark Educational, London, 1988.

5

THE BIG PICTURE ON STRESS

Stress in our life beyond exams

Stress wasn't invented only for exam time. For some of us stress may have already arisen in our earlier lives, including our childhood lives outside of exams. It has been apparent for some time that children need help with stress management and The National Healthy Schools Programme (NHSP) has taken things forward (NHSP, 2006). That venture was jointly funded by education and health departments in the drive to reduce health inequalities, promote social inclusion and raise educational standards.

Keeping young people healthy includes looking after their 'mental health'. This term seems to have drifted into everyday use, although some people may think it sounds a bit heavy. It simply means our sense of well-being, including the way we feel, think, perceive and make sense of our everyday lives. The term, mental health problems, covers a broad range of emotional and behavioural difficulties, including everyday problems such as stress (NHSP, 2006).

The likely causes of stress in young people include a range of widespread and commonly occurring issues in everyday life: divorce and separation; bereavement; domestic violence; parental illness, physical or mental; school problems such as bullying, peer pressure and exams; missing school, including school exclusion; discrimination on grounds such as race, culture, gender, sexuality and disability. Children who are in local authority care are particularly at risk of stress and other mental health problems (NHSP, 2006; Primary Review, 2007).

A significant minority of young people have a fairly severe level of difficulty. One in ten children aged 5–16 years has mental health difficulties described as clinically significant. These range from anxiety, depression, over activity, inattentiveness (ADHD) and anorexia, to conduct disorders such as uncontrollable or destructive behaviour (Layard and Dunn, 2009).

We often rely on adults' appraisals to assess the emotional state of children, but young people themselves are a source of information. In a survey targeting 8,000 youngsters aged 14–16, carried out by The Children's Society in 2005, it was concluded that 27% of young people agreed with the statement, 'I often feel depressed' (Layard and Dunn, 2009). Although there seems to be cause for concern about the emotional state of children and young people, a little caution is needed. Stress information is usually gathered by questionnaires which may simply ask people to tick boxes to say (self report) what is going on in their lives and whether these things are stressful. This type of data is useful and reliable to some extent, but not totally reliable. People are merely giving their views at that time on that day. When people are asked whether they are stressed, some may agree in order to 'go with the flow'. They may be swayed by trends in media and popular lifestyle issues.

Since the 1960s some authors say that there has been a cultural shift which emphasises emotions over intellect and sees human beings as needing help or therapy as a routine part of life (Ecclestone and Hayes, 2009). There may be something in this view but, nonetheless, we all strive to see what is really happening in the lives of young people and we try to help them when they need it. There are plenty of sources of stress around in the lives of young people and we shall look at some of them later in this chapter.

How stress shows itself: our body's reaction

Our body responds when we perceive that something negative such as a threat, burden or irritation is about to spring upon us.

It is important to say that we are not designed for these internal bodily responses to persist for an extended period of time. When our experience of negative events or *thoughts of negative events*, is prolonged, then our body's responses are prolonged, leading to overload. This overload is stress which we can experience in a range of ways, as shown in Figure 5.1.

Some of our bodily responses are described in more detail below. These reactions happen naturally in the body. They may be quite harmless when

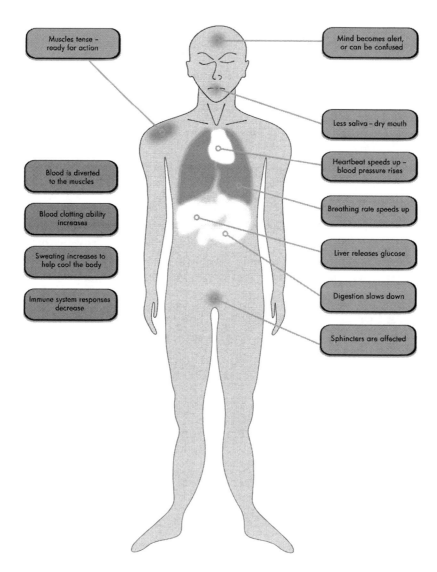

Muscles tense – ready for action

Mind becomes alert, or can be confused

Less saliva – dry mouth

Blood is diverted to the muscles

Heartbeat speeds up – blood pressure rises

Blood clotting ability increases

Breathing rate speeds up

Sweating increases to help cool the body

Liver releases glucose

Immune system responses decrease

Digestion slows down

Sphincters are affected

Figure 5.1 Our body's responses to stress

they happen only for short periods. They become stress, when we experience them repeatedly, or for an extended period of time. Remember that, if you feel stressed from time to time you are not alone. It seems likely that many people experience a degree of stress at some point in their lives.

Muscle tension

When muscle tension is prolonged this can result in discomfort, perhaps to the point of a stiff neck or headaches. Amongst the bodily signs of stress, muscle tension may be amongst the easiest to alleviate through exercises or muscle relaxation.

The digestive system

The digestive system slows down when we are under stress. We may be aware of a stomach churning sensation when stressed. Our appetite may be suppressed with less inclination to eat in the short term. On the other hand, some of us might be more inclined to 'comfort eating' when under stress. We each react to stress with our own distinctive combination of reactions, but any prolonged disruption of our eating habits may not be beneficial.

The immune system

The immune system can be suppressed under stress. We seem more susceptible to colds and other commonplace ailments when under stress. Clearly this would be to our disadvantage were it to continue in the long term.

Heart rate increases

Our tense muscles need more blood and so the heart rate increases to give them more oxygen and more glucose (fuel). This is needed in the short term, but long term high blood pressure may not be good for us.

Sleepless nights

Worrying thoughts keep us awake. One or two sleepless nights may be a commonplace experience but long term sleeplessness can clearly be a drain on our energies.

Poor memory

When adults are under stress we might forget familiar information such as PIN numbers. Perhaps you left your keys somewhere and cannot recall where you put them (in the fridge!). We treat this in a light-hearted way if it does not happen too often, but frequent disruption to memory may amount to an additional source of stress. We may find it frustrating when we forget things such as what we are expected to take to, or bring home from, lectures.

You may already have a good understanding of how stress shows itself in your life before college. Let's start at the beginning and sort out some of the more frequent causes of stress.

Life before college: some of the things that cause stress

- Brothers and sisters – they can really upset you.
- Clothes – I worry if I don't have the latest fashions.
- Examinations – everyone's going to do better than me.
- Family changes – there seems to be a lot of arguing at home.
- Food – I'm worried about fatty food, additives, genetically modified food, meat.
- Good looking – I worry about my looks – it's no good if you're not good looking.
- Gossip – I worry that people are saying nasty things about me.
- Health – I worry about my weight.
- Keeping promises – people don't always do what they say they are going to do.
- Keeping secrets – it's terrible when you tell someone something really private and they tell everyone else.
- Losing a friend – we could still be friends if only …

- Misunderstandings – I didn't know I was supposed to meet her after school and now she won't speak to me.
- Money – how can I get enough or at least get as much as everyone else?
- Older adults – they just don't understand.
- Pressure – people trying to get me to do things which I don't want to do.
- Studying – there's always too much of it.
- Sports – I worry I'm not good at sports.
- Sleep – I can't get to sleep at night or I wake up in the middle of the night and can't get back to sleep again.
- Talking big – hearing other people bragging about things makes me feel left out.
- Social media – everyone seems to be famous and have loads of money. How can I keep up with all that? Does everyone like me?

With plenty of possible 'stressors' or sources of stress around the place it would not be surprising if young people became stressed.

Life before college: stress indicators in school students

When looking back at your school days it may help to try and decide whether you were behaving in a way which indicated your need for help with stress – or was it just the way you are? For example, if you are often arguing with family members, perhaps it's just an adolescent phase. With hindsight you might decide you have grown out of it.

On the other hand, if the arguing is too intense or it carries on over too long a period of time, this may be a sign that you are under stress. Thinking about your life before college, here are some possible stress indicators in school students.

- Difficulties paying attention in class
- Not listening to what others say at home
- Not understanding what the teacher is saying
- Worried about the future – passing exams
- Wanting to miss days at school
- Late for school
- Saying you have too much homework

- Arguing with family members
- Saying you have no friends and feel lonely
- Gaining or losing weight
- Sleeping badly
- Feeling sad
- Stopping the hobbies which you used to enjoy

Most stress writers seem to be agreed that being in a stressed state means we are tense, less adaptable to change, with less ability to think carefully or decide how to go about things and with less capacity to enjoy the 'here and now'. It is not surprising that a stressed state of mind means that we have difficulty listening, studying, have problems getting on with people and disturbed sleep. All of these things seem likely to disrupt a young person's progress. A stress management programme seems like a good idea.

6

WHAT THE EXPERTS SAY ABOUT STRESS

Experts in any field have a need to be precise and define things. As a student you may have a clear idea of what stress is, without any need to define it, but let's go ahead and see what the experts have to say about stress.

A definition of stress

It is important that a definition of stress distinguishes pressure from stress. Stress is defined as, 'The adverse reaction people have to excessive pressure or other types of demand placed upon them' (Health and Safety Executive, 2003). So stress, by definition, means that we are overloaded with too much pressure and no recovery time, taking us beyond our capacity to cope. You may have heard people say that some stress is good for you. Well, it's good to experience a wide range of things in life and so stress may be something you can learn from. Nonetheless stress, by definition, is not good.

The definition above is a definition of work related stress. Nonetheless it is a good definition for everyday stress and so we can use it as a way of defining personal or exam stress.

Experts like theory. They like some sort of unifying system of thought which will explain what's happening and allow us to predict what is going to happen in future. The most often quoted theory of stress is outlined below.

The origin of our stress reactions: fight or flight

Pressure is different from stress. Pressure can be positive, motivating, help us to achieve our goals and perform more effectively. In order to understand the difference between stress and pressure we need to look at the basis for our stress reactions.

In order to explain stress it helps to look at the origin of stress within an ancient survival mechanism which has existed in human beings since the earliest stages of our evolution. This mechanism is referred to as the 'fight or flight' responses, a term often credited to Cannon (1929). For example, Stone Age people, when seeing a threat from a woolly mammoth or sabre toothed tiger, needed to prepare to defend themselves (fight) or escape (flight) from danger. In this fight or flight state the body is ready for intense, short term physical activity.

The brain becomes aware of danger as a result of messages received from the eyes, ears and so on. Hormones are released and the involuntary nervous system sends signals to various parts of the body to produce a range of responses (Open University, 1992).These responses include: muscles tensing ready for action; heart rate increasing ready to fuel the muscles; digestive system winding down because we do not need to eat in the short term; immune system is suppressed because we can manage for a short period without it.

When the body has prepared itself for basic survival behaviour, we are ready to react physically, with a fairly crude and limited range of responses, which essentially involve running away or defending ourselves. We are not in the best state of mind for carefully balanced decision making. Some examples of decision making from our life after college or university might include: whether to take that job; whether to buy that house; whether to marry that person. We need our coolest head and our most balanced sense of judgment for these decisions. Therefore it may be best to avoid, as far as possible, making important and delicate decisions when under stress. When under stress we are not on top form for exercising our subtle skills in areas such as communication and empathy. Listening carefully to a friend's sad story or choosing the curtains are probably best not attempted under stress.

The ancient fight or flight survival mechanisms have remained within us to the present day. Consider what happens inside you when you are driving a car and you have a near miss in traffic. Your reactions are the fight or flight reactions of: heart rate increasing; stomach churning; muscles tensing and so on. How does this help us to understand the difference between stress and pressure?

The difference between stress and pressure

Let's assume that Stone Age people probably faced some level of threat from animals such as a sabre toothed tiger from time to time, but not continuously. In a lifetime you may have had a few near misses in traffic but they do not happen several times a day. The fight or flight responses help us to react, but our bodies are not designed to be maintained continuously in a fight or flight state.

When under pressure we may be stretched to some extent, but we can work within our capacity and build in some recovery time. However pressure can continue for too long or increase its intensity and become excessive. When that happens, pressure moves over a boundary into stress.

Stress management theory

The fight or flight idea does seem a valid explanation of how stress arises. However, it does not explain how to reduce stress. For this the experts have come up with a second set of ideas.

The importance of perception change

In everyday life we may have negative events such as exams actually happening to us and we need to manage the stress associated with these events. Nonetheless stress can be created, not only by real life events. Stress can arise from our thoughts. We can be stressed merely by thinking about negative events.

When we think of something our bodies respond to what we are thinking. For example, when we are hungry and think of food our mouths water. When we think of meeting someone we are fond of, we may tingle with excitement. When we think of a nice holiday we may experience a feeling of well being. This happens with negative experiences too. Let's go back to the example of a near miss in traffic. A few moments after the near miss our bodily reactions may settle down and we continue driving fairly normally. Then we might think again of the near miss. What happens then? Our heart rate increases, muscles tense and so on, all over again. When we think of something stressful, the body reacts in a similar way to actually experiencing the stressful event.

For many of us our negative thinking can be fairly continuous. If we repeatedly think about negative things, we are maintaining our bodies in the flight or fight state. We are not designed for this bodily state to be continuous. Repeatedly putting ourselves into fight or flight mode in the long term, with insufficient chance to recover, can lead to overload and then we are in a state of stress.

When we are under stress, muscle relaxation is not enough for effective stress management. We need to carry out muscle relaxation but, at the same time look at our thinking, our perceptions of our world. Perception change is important in stress alleviation. 'There is nothing good or bad but thinking makes it so' (Hamlet, Act 2, Scene 2). In other words, we have the ability to think a life event into having a positive or negative effect on us. We have a choice to re-think and substitute a positive thought to replace the negative thought. This gives our bodies a break from the stressful effects of negativity.

We do not banish the negative thought completely. We still need to tackle life's problems, find the money to pay that bill, fix the leaking washing machine and so on. Nonetheless we need not be overwhelmed by all the things we have to do. We can think ourselves into having a break from our worries and this re-thinking from negative to pleasant, positive thoughts is what the experts call perception change.

In this programme, perception change is dealt with by the Cognitive Behavioural Approach (CBA). This technique has been developed from the original works of Aaron Beck (1961), Albert Ellis (1955) and Donald Meichenbaum (1974). In this book and the recorded stress management audio tracks, the everyday term we use instead of perception change is 'choosing what to think'.

In other words this programme has been devised using a coherent approach aimed at your achieving robust, long term skills for stress management by applying two theories. First there is muscle relaxation and generally easing our bodily fight or flight reactions. Then the widely accepted CBA method for transforming our thoughts, from negative and stress inducing, to positive and restoring a sense of wellbeing.

Relaxation scripts

Inviting people to listen to a relaxation script, recorded or spoken live, is a widely used method amongst experts in the field of anxiety and stress management. Some scripts rely mainly on muscle relaxation, based on a progressive muscle relaxation technique usually credited to Mitchell (1987). This method has been modified by others to make the muscle relaxation sequences more concise and add other components such as inviting the participant to focus on their own breathing (Palmer and Cooper, 2007).

Many scripts add to the relaxation with visualising a favourite, relaxing place and focusing on its colours, sounds, aromas and so on. Relaxation scripts which provide a carefully structured combination of components including feelings, sensations, imagery and so on may stem from multimodal therapy (Lazarus, 1992).

People are often invited to listen to repeats of the same spoken sequence in a script on the assumption that they will improve with practice, allowing a state of relaxation to be achieved more readily on each successive occasion. Over a period of many years there have been a large number of published relaxation scripts, revisiting familiar themes and it is not always possible to identify the original authors. As with everything else in this programme, the scripts were not invented from scratch. The scripts were devised following the established practice of the experts.

So in this programme you are invited to visualise a nice picture, not only for its relaxing properties, but as an alternative thought, a replacement for your anxiety inducing thought. This is intended as a CBA approach and the term, choosing what to think, is employed to describe an invitation to change your perceptions from stressful to pleasant. Perception change and muscle relaxation are offered together in each of the relaxation scripts.

The scripts develop from Session 1 onwards, and in Session 3 the audio track invites you to take part in a visualisation of 'breathing all your worries into a balloon'. This simple technique is widely used in stress and relaxation manuals (author unknown). You are invited to visualise a balloon, its colour and so on, then inflate it by blowing all your worries into the balloon and letting it float away. This is a method for inviting you to take a break from your worries, by putting the release from your worries into a tangible, visual form.

The experts use a wide range of stress reduction visualisations. For example some scripts are written around fairly broad, quality of life issues such as visualising yourself taking up a different viewpoint, several years into the future and seeing whether your problems are less stressful from that perspective (Palmer and Cooper, 2007). Such strategies invite the person into an imaginary structure where they can calmly reflect on their situation and explore stress solutions through their own creativity.

7

STUDENTS RELAXING TOGETHER

Sharing something is enjoyable and valuable. This principle applies to helping each other with difficulties as well as letting our friends know about the good times.

Why do stress management together?

When a small group of three or four students relaxes together, that sharing adds to the motivation to do more relaxation sessions. You can motivate each other. When one person is feeling a bit flat the others can be sympathetic and encourage joining in.

After each track has finished the group can talk about how it felt to relax, the pleasant thoughts which each person chose and the feelings which went with those thoughts. This conversation is another opportunity for sharing as a group.

What's in the five relaxation scripts?

Each audio track talks you through whatever pleasant thought you have chosen. The audio gives guidance to students on how to accentuate, enhance or clarify their pleasant thoughts. The audio recordings are 'non-directive', in other words the recordings are not written along the lines of, 'Think of a sunny day on the beach.' Your most recent memory of a beach might be sunburn – not relaxing at all. This general style of wording helps to reduce the risk that any image suggested by an outsider might not be relaxing.

Start Session 1 by listening to relaxation audio Track 1. This track invites participants to think of a 'nice picture' or see a nice picture in their mind's eye. This allows the same script wording to be used for everybody, individually or in a group. Each person chooses a picture which suits their mood and preferences.

Track 2 repeats the script of Track 1 and then adds a new component by inviting people to think of a nice phrase or saying such as, 'Tomorrow is another day' or 'The sun will still shine tomorrow.' These examples of phrases are given to prompt participants and show that a simple, short phrase may be best but the wording is non-directive again so people can choose any saying which suits them.

The invitation to think of a nice picture, then a nice phrase or saying is repeated in successive tracks. This repetition is intentional. It is important and it is not a 'filler'. Repetition gives you practice at the skills of relaxation plus choosing what to think. Just like any other task in life, we each start off at a different level of competence. If we were all to sit down to have our first piano lesson some of us would be better than others right from the start. Those of us who were less skillful would improve with practice. It is the same with relaxation skills. We each vary as to how good we are at relaxation, and practice helps us to improve our relaxation skills. Table 7.1 shows how the relaxation scripts develop.

In successive tracks the 'choosing what to think' wording of the script changes to provide a developing stress management sequence. For example in Track 3, 'Breathe all your worries into a balloon', the wording invites you to see all your worries floating away for a while. This enables you to take a break from your worries and return refreshed to deal with whatever you have to do.

Table 7.1   The five relaxation scripts in summary

Session 1	Session 2	Session 3	Session 4	Session 5 Exam stress
Listen to audio Track 1, which invites you, in the order below, to	Listen to audio Track 2, which invites you, in the order below, to	Listen to audio Track 3, which invites you, in the order below, to	Listen to audio Track 4, which invites you, in the order below, to	Listen to audio Track 5, which invites you, in the order below, to
choose to think:	choose to think:	choose to think:	choose to think:	choose to think:
I relax my muscles	I relax my muscles	I relax my muscles	I relax my muscles	I relax my muscles
about a nice picture	about a nice picture	about a nice picture	about a nice picture	about a nice picture
	about a nice phrase or saying	about a nice phrase or saying	about a nice phrase or saying	about a nice phrase or saying and then …
		I breathe all my worries into a balloon	I can see myself in my mind's eye, helping a stressed person	I touch myself on the wrist [as a portable relaxation reminder for use outside the session]

In Track 4, seeing in your mind's eye a stressed person whom you can help, is intended to take your mind off your own stresses by 'taking you out of yourself'. In doing this you may begin to see yourself as a resource, as someone with a contribution to make, as someone worthwhile, resilient instead of vulnerable to stress.

Session 5 is the exam stress session. The touch on the wrist is designed as a portable relaxation reminder for use outside the audio sessions in situations such as travelling to and starting exams. Nonetheless it is widely applicable to other situations where people may find it valuable such as: public speaking; just before you have to take your turn to speak in a lecture or tutorial; when you're worried about a rumour; when someone seems to ignore you; offensive behaviour from another driver on a public road. The touch on the wrist relaxation can be used as a quick way of managing stress at any time in a wide range of locations.

You cannot start your audio listening with Session 5. You need to learn relaxation and choosing what to think skills in Sessions 1–4 before embarking on Session 5.

8

I AM TOO BUSY FOR STRESS MANAGEMENT

It is easy to tell ourselves that we are too busy juggling our lives to set aside time to manage the stress which can result from being too busy and having, or maybe choosing to take on more things than we can handle. It may be that most people reading this will have heard of useful ways to manage stress such as prioritising your jobs, building in some 'downtime', take exercise and so on. It is worth repeating that knowing about the existence of these techniques does not give you the motivation to put them into practice. You may know how to handle stress but not have the drive to do anything about it.

Little time or effort needed

In this programme it takes around 15–20 minutes to complete one session. You might typically carry out one session per week and there are five sessions to complete the course. You add to that the few minutes it takes to read the short Chapter 1, which is a summary of background information on stress management. If you were to do your own cost–benefit analysis, this programme might show up quite well.

Little effort is needed. After reading the first few pages, all you need do is sit and listen to an audio relaxation track and follow what it says.

Built in motivation

This programme has motivation built into it to take you to Session 2 and onwards, as you will see in Figure 8.1.

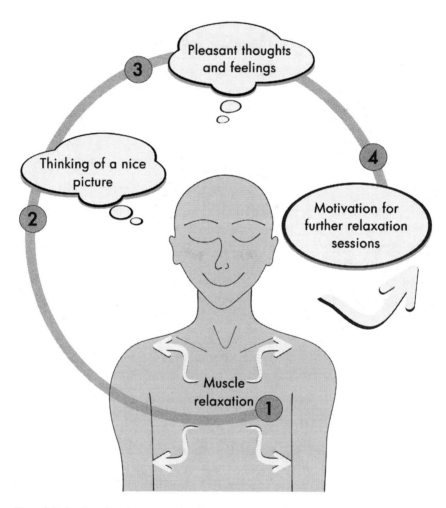

Figure 8.1 Session 1 activates motivation

Relaxation involving pleasant thoughts and feelings can be enjoyable and the enjoyment can provide the motivation to take part in a second session and so on after that. The pleasant and positive start to this programme motivates you to repeat the pleasant experience by taking part in further sessions.

Session 2 gives you more nice thoughts and feelings which again motivate you to take part in the next relaxation session and so on to Session 5.

9

CHOOSING WHAT TO THINK

What is the point of sitting around thinking of a nice picture? Basically because, when you think of something the body responds to what you are thinking. If you think of something scary your body tenses up. If you think of something pleasant your body relaxes. Choosing what to think, as we call it, or perception change, as the experts describe it, is a crucial part of stress management.

Of all the body's stress reactions, sweating, stomach churning and so on, muscle tension may be the easiest to focus on. So relaxing your muscles is a good initial stress reduction technique. But this is not enough on its own.

It is worth repeating that this programme is not being made up as we go along. Your life is too important for you to spend time reading one author's ideas on how to manage your stress. The contribution of this book is an attempt to simplify the ideas of some major thinkers on human nature, distil them down and pass them on to you. This programme is worthwhile because it is based on the work of authentic psychologists which has stood the test of time.

Figure 9.1 below gives you an idea of the psychology behind the choosing-what-to-think approach. To get going, start at top centre of the diagram, look at thoughts (cognition) and go round clockwise.

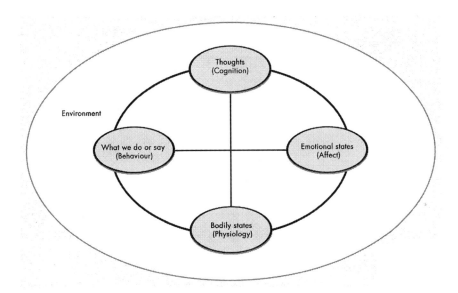

Figure 9.1 Basic design of the Cognitive Behavioural Approach
Sources: Padesky & Mooney, 1990.; Westbrook, Kennerley & Kirk, 2007.

Our thoughts such as 'I am not going to do well in my exam' lead to emotions such as anxiety. Our anxiety leads to a change in bodily state, stomach churning for example. Stomach churning affects our behaviour such as being distracted by a feeling of nausea and not listening to what is being taught in a lecture or lesson.

In managing stress we need to change that sequence. We choose to think of a nice picture, which leads to feelings such as wellbeing. Our feeling of wellbeing leads to a change in bodily state such as muscle relaxation. Relaxation affects our behaviour and allows us to change our focus from a worry about the future to experiencing the here and now, concentrating and taking in information.

When we get past Session 4, choosing what to think is more refined, as shown in Figure 9.2. This time the thought moves up from a simple picture or saying to choosing to think of helping a stressed person. The stress management rationale is that lower stress leads to a greater sense of wellbeing,

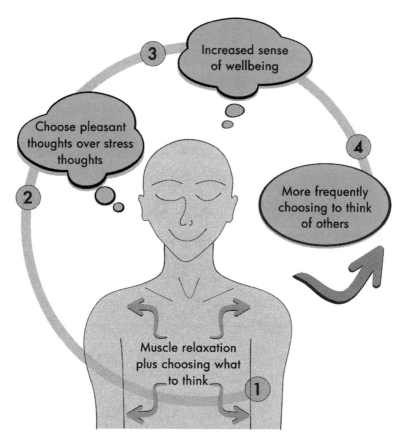

Figure 9.2 Session 4 can enhance engagement with others

which is liberating and opens the door to thinking about other people, freeing us from thinking about ourselves and our own stress.

From thinking less about ourselves to more frequent thinking of others we become more engaged with others and we are more fulfilled. That in turn gives us the potential to build a life as we really want it, with more fulfilment and less stress. Rather than dealing with individual stresses as they arise we can build a lifestyle where we are less likely to encounter stress.

Stress management as a practical philosophy of life

You may find Figure 9.3 helpful in summarising how we move from rushing around juggling and 'fire fighting', to getting a firm grip and a

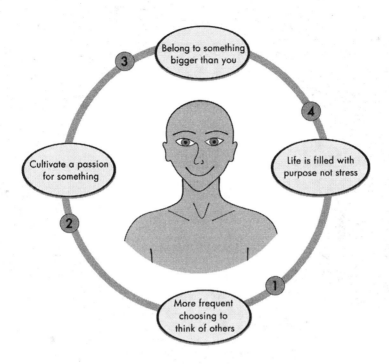

Figure 9.3 A low stress philosophy

calm approach to life in the long term. When we choose to think pleasant thoughts, when pleasant feelings follow, it's easier to think beyond ourselves, think more about our family, the wider community and about helping others who may be stressed or disadvantaged in some way.

Choosing to think of helping one person can lead to a range of positive and helpful activities. Helping a frail person with their garden may lead to a passion for gardening and then belonging to something bigger than you such as a local gardening association which helps frail people throughout the community. We become less focused on ourselves and more engaged with others. Stress has been replaced with thriving interaction between the needy and the resourceful. Our life becomes more meaningful and purpose-driven not stress-driven.

10

UNPACKING THE PHILOSOPHY

The rationale of this programme is to try and go a bit deeper into stress management, beyond essential oils and pamper sessions, chocolate and a bottle of wine in front of the TV, or drinking with your crowd. Although such things may have their place, used in moderation, as part of a balanced approach to life, they are likely to be short term comforts rather than real stress management. An authentic stress management programme can help you to build long term peace of mind.

Helping a stressed person: what's that about?

As well as trying to treat you as an individual, this programme has an angle, a rationale, a philosophy, if you don't mind that term. The relaxation scripts follow the rationale of changing the focus of attention away from anxiety inducing thoughts on to something relaxing, in other words, choosing what to think. However after the initial 'nice picture in your mind's eye' audio tracks, we are invited in Session 4 to see ourselves helping a stressed person. Let's unpack what this has got to do with us and our stress.

The idea behind wording an audio track around helping a stressed person was set off when I once heard Dr Anthony Clare, psychiatrist, talking on the radio as part of a series of interviews he conducted with a wide range of celebrities. Dr Clare went beyond eliciting mere anecdotes from his interviewees. He dug a bit deeper and indeed he had plenty of experience to draw upon. He was a thinker, author, medical director of a hospital and university professor. During one of his broadcasts he said something along the lines that stress is reduced when we cultivate a passion for something and belong to something bigger than us. The author had been involved in stress management for many years by that time. Those words made an impact and led to reflection and reading around what he had said.

Meaning and purpose in our lives

From time to time you might hear the older people in your life talking about their younger lives when they had passions for many things such as political change, music and going to live concerts, drama and getting embroiled in all the latest plays and films, or literature and devouring novels every week. What happened to all that?

Back in the day, when the older people you know were, say, in their twenties or thirties, their enthusiasm for a cause may have led to membership of a political party or environmental organisation. How did they stop getting enthusiastic about joining in? Stress can have that effect on us by draining our energy, limiting our vision and our thinking about what life can be.

It made sense to say that cultivating or re-cultivating a passion and belonging to something bigger than us would add meaning and purpose to our lives. When our lives have purpose, for example when we are building something in life, showing commitment to something in life, we are less likely to be governed by the to-do list, the school run, the diet, social media or 'reality' television. When our lives are filled with purpose we are less likely to be filled with anxiety and stress.

Reading around stress led to re-visiting the work of psychologists who had first published many years ago. For example, there was Maslow, whose approach was to focus on the positives of personal development rather than the negatives or conditions which need to be treated. For example, if someone is anxious about getting into a lift we might be a bit too ready to respond by dishing out a label and saying they have claustrophobia. Does the label really help? Maslow might have said that anxieties about entering a lift could be better dealt with by helping the person to develop qualities such as courage and perseverance. Maslow's intention might have been to show people that there is an alternative. People are not static. Your mind is not a medical condition on legs. People grow, develop, become self-aware, concerned with personal growth, less concerned with the opinions of others and interested in fulfilling their potential (Maslow, 1954).

The work of Maslow and others helped to lay the foundations for positive psychology. In the past, mainstream psychology has tended to be rather negative, focusing on human weaknesses such as anxiety, fear, anger, depression, creating syndromes and trying to find their remedies. Instead of going down that road we could nurture human qualities such as courage, altruism, honesty, faith, duty, responsibility, good cheer and perseverance (Seligman, 2000).

Positive psychology has given us a steer on what psychology has to say about what makes life worth living (Peterson and Park, 2003). There is an emphasis on fulfilment, not treatment, acquiring a sense of direction and building resilience, not treating dysfunction (Deci and Ryan, 2000). All this seems relevant to stress management. When we are under stress we do not want 'treatment'. We want to learn strategies which build our resilience to stress. We want to find out how we can overcome stress and share our success with those around us.

Looking a little further at positive psychology we can see that a low stress, 'happy' state of mind is achieved in three ways. At first we experience pleasant emotions, but these are transient and rely on our being in the right situation with nothing going too wrong in life. The second involves engaging in activities and social relationships so that we 'lose ourselves'. The third involves achieving meaning, purpose and fulfilment in life. The idea is to aim for all three states but with greater emphasis on engagement and meaning (Peterson, Park and Seligman, 2005; Richards, Rivers and Akhurst, 2008).

How could all this be built into a stress management programme? The relaxation audio scripts follow the first two steps of that sequence. First step: experiencing pleasant emotions by relaxing and seeing a nice picture in our mind's eye. Second step: 'losing ourselves' in stepping outside ourselves and visualising ourselves helping a stressed person. If we imagine ourselves helping a stressed person, there is a possibility that we might take the next step of helping someone in real life. When we do so, this involves thinking of another person, putting our own stress to one side, losing ourselves and engaging with someone else. The door is then open to the third stage, which may be addressed more fully in a future set of scripts, making the engagement stronger by cultivating a passion for something and belonging to something bigger than us. This engagement in a community of some sort enables meaning and purpose in life.

The here and now

In this programme the combination of relaxation plus guided positive thoughts is akin to 'mindfulness', which may have its origins in meditation practices from other cultures. Nowadays these activities have moved on to become established as relatively mainstream techniques in western civilisations.

As with everything else in this programme, none of the ideas originate with the author. Rather it brings together some of the best theory and practice from psychology in a straightforward manner which is easily accessed and not too time consuming.

On a wider scale, beyond this programme, a combination of CBA and mindfulness is considered to be valuable and effective. The Mental Health Foundation (MHF, 2010) has launched a report in response to the growing evidence for, and popularity of mindfulness. That report examines the evidence for the effectiveness of mindfulness-based therapies, lays the groundwork for using these therapies within the NHS and beyond and explores the potential knock-on effects for society at large. The combination of CBA and meditation is well established in the UK. An online course is offered by MHF which contains the core elements of Mindfulness-Based Stress Reduction (MBSR) and Mindfulness-Based Cognitive Therapy (MBCT) www.bemindfulonline.com That course has been evaluated and found to be effective. Participation in the online mindfulness course significantly reduced perceived stress upon completion and results remained stable at follow-up (Krusche, Cyhlarova, King and Williams, 2012).

The audio tracks can help people to pay attention to the present moment rather than get stressed about what has happened or what might happen. The combination of scripts plus muscle relaxation follows the mindfulness rationale in helping us to become more aware of body sensations, thoughts and feelings. Repeated negative thoughts can put our body into stress mode. A few moments relaxation can help us to detect that we are under stress and provide an opportunity to replace worrying thoughts with pleasant thoughts. This gives us a break from our worries so that we can re-charge our batteries and approach our problems anew. A state of relaxation provides a good foundation for choosing what to think.

Where next?

The author is assuming, and inviting you to share the assumption, that we see the potential for development in our lives when we interact more frequently and more meaningfully with others. This engagement is both an indication that we are managing our stress and a means of deepening our experience of life by pouring in fulfilment and letting go stress. When our interaction with others develops into a real sense of community, '… a soft quietness develops. It is a kind of peace.' (Peck, 1988, p.103). That sounds like successful stress management. Wouldn't you agree?

THE RELAXATION SCRIPTS

If you are doing relaxation in a small group, as you become more familiar with the way in which the relaxation scripts are read in the recording, one of you may like to try reading the scripts yourself. You might find it fun to do and you may be able to read the scripts in a style which suits your group better than the recorded style. Here are the five scripts.

Script for the relaxation recording: Track 1

Get comfortable in your seat, or you can lie down on the floor if you want to.

There is no talking during the relaxation which we are going to do in a moment.

I am going to invite you to relax.

All you have to do is listen to what I say.

I am going to speak quite slowly to make it easier for you to take in what I am saying and relax along with me.

I am going to count out loud, counting down from ten to one.

After each number I count you can become a bit more relaxed.

When I get to number one you can feel very, very relaxed.

10-9-8-7-6-5-4-3-2-1, very relaxed, very, very relaxed.

Now I am going to say some things to relax us a bit more.

If you choose to, you can now say inside your own head, 'I relax my toes.'

That's it. I'm inviting you to choose what to think.

When you think of something, your body can respond to what you are thinking.

You can choose to think, 'I relax my toes.'

If you choose to think, 'I relax my toes,' your toes can relax.

As your toes relax, notice any changes in the feelings in your toes as they relax.

Notice if your toes become warm, tingly or cool.

Notice if your toes appear light in weight, or heavy in weight.

Whatever the feelings in your toes, as your toes relax, notice the feelings.

Now we can do more choosing what to think.

If you choose to, think inside your head, 'I relax all the muscles in my feet.'

When you think of something, your body can respond to what you are thinking.

When you choose to think, 'I relax all the muscles in my feet,' your feet muscles can relax.

Notice any changes in the feelings in your feet muscles as they relax.

Notice if your feet become warm, tingly or cool.

Notice if your feet appear light in weight, or heavy in weight.

Whatever the feelings in your feet, as your feet relax, notice the feelings.

You may choose to think of some of your other muscles and relax those too.

You may choose to think, 'I relax all my leg muscles, all my back muscles, all my stomach muscles.'

Those muscles can then relax.

Then relax your neck muscles.

Then relax your shoulder muscles.

Then relax your jaw muscles.

Then go on like that, relaxing all the muscles in your body.

Or if you prefer, you may choose to think, 'I relax all the muscles in my body.'

If you choose, you can relax all your muscles at the same time. It is as simple as that.

Allow the relaxation to flow throughout your body.

Notice any changes in the feelings in your muscles as your body relaxes.

Allow the weight of your body to sink a little deeper into the chair, or into the floor.

If you wish to change your body position to be more comfortable at any stage, then you can do so.

Notice whether you have developed a strong and steady pattern of breathing.

If you have closed your eyes, that is good.

Your body is relaxing.

If you have not yet closed your eyes, now is a good time to close your eyes, if you choose to do so.

As you continue to relax you can continue to hear any routine sounds which may, or may not, take place inside or outside the room.

If you choose to, allow to come into your mind's eye a nice picture of some sort.

The picture may be any nice picture; any nice picture at all.

The picture may be indoors or outside.

The picture may be any nice picture you have in your memory.

The picture may be something nice from today or a few days ago.

Or perhaps your nice picture may be from a long time ago.

You may be able to see your picture clearly or not clearly.

Your picture may look hazy and a bit out of focus.

It doesn't matter if the picture is not too clear in your mind's eye.

Your picture may be a moving picture, like on TV, or it may be a still picture like a photograph.

Your picture may be in colour or it may be in black and white.

There may be people in the picture or there may be no people.

Notice the nice feelings inside you that go with the nice picture.

Notice whereabouts in your body your nice feelings are located.

Perhaps your nice feelings may be located in your stomach, or in your head.

Some people have their nice feelings all over their bodies.

Just stay as you are relaxing nicely for a few more moments

Relaxing for a few more moments

Relaxing for a few more moments

Relaxing for a few more moments

In a moment I am going to count out loud from one to ten.

When I say the number ten, keeping hold of your calm feelings, open your
    eyes, be refreshed and feel alert as usual.

1-2-3-4-5-6-7-8-9-10.

Open your eyes.

You are now refreshed, fully alert and ready to do everything as usual.

You are now refreshed, fully alert and ready to do everything as usual.

End of Session

Script for the relaxation recording: Track 2

Get comfortable in your seat, or you can lie down on the floor if you want to.

There is no talking during the relaxation which we are going to do in a
    moment.

I am going to invite you to relax.

All you have to do is listen to what I say.

I am going to speak quite slowly to make it easier for you to take in what I
    am saying and relax along with me.

I am going to count out loud, counting down from ten to one.

After each number I count you can become a bit more relaxed.

When I get to number one you can feel very, very relaxed.

10-9-8-7-6-5-4-3-2-1, very relaxed, very, very relaxed.

Now I am going to say some things to relax us a bit more.

If you choose to, you can now say inside your own head, 'I relax my toes.'

That's it. I'm inviting you to choose what to think.

When you think of something, your body can respond to what you are
    thinking.

You can choose to think, 'I relax my toes.'

If you choose to think, 'I relax my toes,' your toes can relax.

As your toes relax, notice any changes in the feelings in your toes as they relax.

Notice if your toes become warm, tingly or cool.

Notice if your toes appear light in weight, or heavy in weight.

Whatever the feelings in your toes, as your toes relax, notice the feelings.

Now we can do more choosing what to think.

If you choose to, think inside your head, 'I relax all the muscles in my feet.'

When you think of something, your body can respond to what you are thinking.

When you choose to think, 'I relax all the muscles in my feet,' your feet muscles can relax.

Notice any changes in the feelings in your feet muscles as they relax.

Notice if your feet become warm, tingly or cool.

Notice if your feet appear light in weight, or heavy in weight.

Whatever the feelings in your feet, as your feet relax, notice the feelings.

You may choose to think of some of your other muscles and relax those too.

You may choose to think, 'I relax all my leg muscles, all my back muscles, all my stomach muscles.'

Those muscles can then relax.

Then relax your neck muscles.

Then relax your shoulder muscles.

Then relax your jaw muscles.

Then go on like that, relaxing all the muscles in your body.

Or if you prefer, you may choose to think, 'I relax all the muscles in my body.'

If you choose, you can relax all your muscles at the same time. It is as simple as that.

Allow the relaxation to flow throughout your body.

Notice any changes in the feelings in your muscles as your body relaxes.

Allow the weight of your body to sink a little deeper into the chair, or into the floor.

If you wish to change your body position to be more comfortable at any stage, then you can do so.

Notice whether you have developed a strong and steady pattern of breathing.

If you have closed your eyes; that is good.

Your body is relaxing.

If you have not yet closed your eyes, now is a good time to close your eyes, if you choose to do so.

As you continue to relax you can continue to hear any routine sounds which may, or may not, take place inside or outside the room.

If you choose to, allow to come into your mind's eye a nice picture of some sort.
The picture may be any nice picture; any nice picture at all.
The picture may be indoors or outside.
The picture may be any nice picture you have in your memory.
The picture may be something nice from today or a few days ago.
Or perhaps your nice picture may be from a long time ago.
You may be able to see your picture clearly, or not clearly.
Your picture may look hazy and a bit out of focus.
It doesn't matter if the picture is not too clear in your mind's eye.
Your picture may be a moving picture, like on TV, or it may be a still picture like a photograph.
Your picture may be in colour or it may be in black and white.
There may be people in the picture or there may be no people.

Notice the nice feelings inside you that go with the nice picture.
Notice whereabouts in your body your nice feelings are located.
Perhaps your nice feelings may be located in your stomach, or in your head.
Some people have their nice feelings all over their bodies.

Keep the nice picture in your mind's eye for a few moments longer.
Keep your nice feelings while you think of a nice phrase or saying.
Choose one nice phrase or saying to say inside your head.
Such as: 'Tomorrow is another day'; or 'Every cloud has a silver lining'; or 'The sun will still shine tomorrow.'
Or choose a saying of your own.

Repeat for a few moments your nice phrase or saying inside your head.
Notice the nice feelings inside you that go with the nice phrase or saying.
Notice whereabouts in your body your nice feelings are located.
Perhaps your nice feelings may be located in your stomach, or in your head.
Some people have their nice feelings all over their bodies.

Just stay as you are relaxing nicely for a few more moments.
Relaxing for a few more moments.
Relaxing for a few more moments.
Relaxing for a few more moments.

In a moment I am going to count out loud from one to ten.

When I say the number ten, keeping hold of your calm feelings, open your eyes, be refreshed and feel alert as usual.

1-2-3-4-5-6-7-8-9-10.

Open your eyes.

You are now refreshed, fully alert and ready to do everything as usual.

You are now refreshed, fully alert and ready to do everything as usual.

End of Session

Script for the relaxation recording: Track 3

Get comfortable in your seat, or you can lie down on the floor if you want to.

There is no talking during the relaxation which we are going to do in a moment.

I am going to invite you to relax.

All you have to do is listen to what I say.

I am going to speak quite slowly to make it easier for you to take in what I am saying and relax along with me.

I am going to count out loud, counting down from ten to one.

After each number I count you can become a bit more relaxed.

When I get to number one you can feel very, very relaxed.

10-9-8-7-6-5-4-3-2-1, very relaxed, very, very relaxed.

Now I am going to say some things to relax us a bit more.

If you choose to, you can now say inside your own head, 'I relax my toes.'

That's it. I'm inviting you to choose what to think.

When you think of something, your body can respond to what you are thinking.

You can choose to think, 'I relax my toes.'

If you choose to think, 'I relax my toes,' your toes can relax.

As your toes relax, notice any changes in the feelings in your toes as they relax.

Notice if your toes become warm, tingly or cool.

Notice if your toes appear light in weight, or heavy in weight.

Whatever the feelings in your toes, as your toes relax, notice the feelings.

Now we can do more choosing what to think.

If you choose to, think inside your head, 'I relax all the muscles in my feet.'

When you think of something, your body can respond to what you are thinking.

When you choose to think, 'I relax all the muscles in my feet,' your feet muscles can relax.

Notice any changes in the feelings in your feet muscles as they relax.

Notice if your feet become warm, tingly or cool.

Notice if your feet appear light in weight, or heavy in weight.

Whatever the feelings in your feet, as your feet relax, notice the feelings.

You may choose to think of some of your other muscles and relax those too.

You may choose to think, 'I relax all my leg muscles, all my back muscles, all my stomach muscles.'

Those muscles can then relax.

Then relax your neck muscles.

Then relax your shoulder muscles.

Then relax your jaw muscles.

Then go on like that, relaxing all the muscles in your body.

Or if you prefer, you may choose to think, 'I relax all the muscles in my body.'

If you choose, you can relax all your muscles at the same time. It is as simple as that.

Allow the relaxation to flow throughout your body.

Notice any changes in the feelings in your muscles as your body relaxes.

Allow the weight of your body to sink a little deeper into the chair, or into the floor.

If you wish to change your body position to be more comfortable at any stage, then you can do so.

Notice whether you have developed a strong and steady pattern of breathing.

If you have closed your eyes, that is good.

Your body is relaxing.

If you have not yet closed your eyes, now is a good time to close your eyes, if you choose to do so.

As you continue to relax you can continue to hear any routine sounds which may, or may not, take place inside or outside the room.

If you choose to, allow to come into your mind's eye a nice picture of some sort.

The picture may be any nice picture; any nice picture at all.

The picture may be indoors or outside.

The picture may be any nice picture you have in your memory.

The picture may be something nice from today or a few days ago.

Or perhaps your nice picture may be from a long time ago.

You may be able to see your picture clearly or not clearly.

Your picture may look hazy and a bit out of focus.

It doesn't matter if the picture is not too clear in your mind's eye.

Your picture may be a moving picture, like on TV, or it may be a still picture like a photograph.

Your picture may be in colour or it may be in black and white.

There may be people in your picture or there may be no people.

Notice the nice feelings inside you that go with the nice picture.

Notice whereabouts in your body your nice feelings are located.

Perhaps your nice feelings may be located in your stomach or in your head.

Some people have their nice feelings all over their bodies.

Keep the nice picture in your mind's eye for a few moments longer.

Keep your nice feelings while you think of a nice phrase or saying.

Choose one nice phrase or saying to say inside your head.

Such as: 'Tomorrow is another day'; or 'Every cloud has a silver lining'; or 'The sun will still shine tomorrow.'

Or choose a saying of your own.

Repeat for a few moments your nice phrase or saying inside your head.

Notice the nice feelings inside that go with the nice phrase or saying.

Notice whereabouts in your body your nice feelings are located.

Perhaps your nice feelings may be located in your stomach or in your head.

Some people have their nice feelings all over their bodies.

In a moment I will tell you of a way of sending away for a while your worries, your worried feelings.

In your mind's eye you may choose to think that you can see a toy balloon which you are holding in your hand.

You have not yet breathed into the balloon.

It looks small and flat in your hand.

Decide what colour it is: red, yellow, blue perhaps, or another colour.

Choose whatever colour you wish it to be, or a mixture of colours.

This balloon is very easy to breathe into.

You need only to breathe into it a few times and it will be full of your breath; as big as it can be.

In your mind's eye, put the balloon to your mouth.

Breathe all your worries into the balloon.

It's easy.

Just breathe in through your nostrils and out through your mouth a few times.

And the balloon is full; as big as it can be.

All your worries are now inside the balloon.

Just breathe in through your nostrils and out through your mouth a few times.

And the balloon is full of your breath.

All your worries are now inside the balloon.

Just breathe in through your nostrils and out through your mouth a few times.

And the balloon is full; as big as it can be.

All your worries are now inside the balloon.

In your mind's eye, take the balloon from your mouth.

Tie a knot in the opening of the balloon to stop your worries coming out.

Let the balloon go – up, up, up and away into the sky.

All your worries have floated away for now.

All your worries have floated away for now.

All your worries have floated away for now.

Just stay as you are relaxing nicely for a few more moments.

Relaxing for a few more moments.

Relaxing for a few more moments.

Relaxing for a few more moments.

In a moment I am going to count out loud from one to ten.

When I say the number ten, keeping hold of your calm feelings, open your eyes, be refreshed and feel alert as usual.

1-2-3-4-5-6-7-8-9-10.

Open your eyes.

You are now refreshed, fully alert and ready to do everything as usual.

You are now refreshed, fully alert and ready to do everything as usual.

End of Session

Script for the relaxation recording: Track 4

Get comfortable in your seat, or you can lie down on the floor if you want to.
There is no talking during the relaxation which we are going to do in a
    moment.
I am going to invite you to relax.
All you have to do is listen to what I say.
I am going to speak quite slowly to make it easier for you to take in what I
    am saying and relax along with me.
I am going to count out loud, counting down from ten to one.
After each number I count you can become a bit more relaxed.
When I get to number one you can feel very, very relaxed.
10-9-8-7-6-5-4-3-2-1, very relaxed, very, very relaxed.

Now I am going to say some things to relax us a bit more.
If you choose to, you can now say inside your own head, 'I relax my toes.'
That's it. I'm inviting you to choose what to think.
When you think of something, your body can respond to what you are
    thinking.
You can choose to think, 'I relax my toes.'
If you choose to think, 'I relax my toes,' your toes can relax.
As your toes relax, notice any changes in the feelings in your toes as they relax.
Notice if your toes become warm, tingly or cool.
Notice if your toes appear light in weight, or heavy in weight.
Whatever the feelings in your toes, as your toes relax, notice the feelings.

Now we can do more choosing what to think.
If you choose to, think inside your head, 'I relax all the muscles in my feet.'
When you think of something, your body can respond to what you are
    thinking.
When you choose to think, 'I relax all the muscles in my feet,' your feet
    muscles can relax.
Notice any changes in the feelings in your feet muscles as they relax.

Notice if your feet become warm, tingly or cool.
Notice if your feet appear light in weight, or heavy in weight.
Whatever the feelings in your feet, as your feet relax, notice the feelings.

You may choose to think of some of your other muscles and relax those too.
You may choose to think, 'I relax all my leg muscles, all my back muscles, all my stomach muscles.'
Those muscles can then relax.
Then relax your neck muscles.
Then relax your shoulder muscles.
Then relax your jaw muscles.
Then go on like that, relaxing all the muscles in your body.
Or if you prefer, you may choose to think, 'I relax all the muscles in my body.'
If you choose, you can relax all your muscles at the same time. It is as simple as that.

Allow the relaxation to flow throughout your body.
Notice any changes in the feelings in your muscles as your body relaxes.
Allow the weight of your body to sink a little deeper into the chair, or into the floor.
If you wish to change your body position to be more comfortable at any stage, then you can do so.
Notice whether you have developed a strong and steady pattern of breathing.
If you have closed your eyes, that is good.
Your body is relaxing.
If you have not yet closed your eyes, now is a good time to close your eyes, if you choose to do so.

As you continue to relax you can continue to hear any routine sounds which may, or may not, take place inside or outside the room.

If you choose to, allow to come into your mind's eye a nice picture of some sort.
The picture may be any nice picture; any nice picture at all.
The picture may be indoors or outside.
The picture may be any nice picture you have in your memory.
The picture may be something nice from today or a few days ago.
Or perhaps your nice picture may be from a long time ago.

You may be able to see your picture clearly or not clearly.
Your picture may look hazy and a bit out of focus.
It doesn't matter if the picture is not too clear in your mind's eye.
Your picture may be a moving picture, like on TV, or it may be a still picture like a photograph.
Your picture may be in colour or it may be in black and white.
There may be people in your picture or there may be no people.

Notice the nice feelings inside you that go with the nice picture.
Notice whereabouts in your body your nice feelings are located.
Perhaps your nice feelings may be located in your stomach or in your head.
Some people have their nice feelings all over their bodies.

Keep the nice picture in your mind's eye for a few moments longer.
Keep your nice feelings while you think of a nice phrase or saying.
Choose one nice phrase or saying to say inside your head.
Such as: 'Tomorrow is another day'; or 'Every cloud has a silver lining'; or 'The sun will still shine tomorrow.'
Or choose a saying of your own.

Repeat for a few moments, your nice phrase or saying inside your head.
Notice the nice feelings inside you that go with the nice phrase or saying.
Notice whereabouts in your body your nice feelings are located.
Perhaps your nice feelings may be located in your stomach, or in your head.
Some people have their nice feelings all over their bodies.

If you choose to, see yourself in your mind's eye helping a stressed person.
See who the stressed person is.
Perhaps someone you know, or someone you have never seen before.
See where the person is, indoors or outside, perhaps in a shop or driving a car, or in a park.
See what the person is doing.
You may be able to see that the person looks or sounds stressed.
See what you are doing or saying to help that person.

Just stay as you are relaxing nicely for a few more moments.
Relaxing for a few more moments.
Relaxing for a few more moments.

Relaxing for a few more moments.

In a moment I am going to count out loud from one to ten.
When I say the number ten, keeping hold of your calm feelings, open your
    eyes, be refreshed and feel alert as usual.
1-2-3-4-5-6-7-8-9-10.
Open your eyes.
You are now refreshed, fully alert and ready to do everything as usual.
You are now refreshed, fully alert and ready to do everything as usual.

End of Session

Script for the relaxation recording: Track 5

Get comfortable in your seat, or you can lie down on the floor if you want to.
There is no talking during the relaxation which we are going to do in a
    moment.
I am going to invite you to relax.
All you have to do is listen to what I say.
I am going to speak quite slowly to make it easier for you to take in what I
    am saying and relax along with me.
I am going to count out loud, counting down from ten to one.
After each number I count you can become a bit more relaxed.
When I get to number one you can feel very, very relaxed.
10-9-8-7-6-5-4-3-2-1, very relaxed, very, very relaxed.

Now I am going to say some things to relax us a bit more.
If you choose to, you can now say inside your own head, 'I relax my toes.'
That's it. I'm inviting you to choose what to think.
When you think of something, your body can respond to what you are
    thinking.
You can choose to think, 'I relax my toes.'
If you choose to think, 'I relax my toes,' your toes can relax.
As your toes relax, notice any changes in the feelings in your toes as they
    relax.
Notice if your toes become warm, tingly or cool.
Notice if your toes appear light in weight, or heavy in weight.
Whatever the feelings in your toes, as your toes relax, notice the feelings.

Now we can do more choosing what to think.

If you choose to, think inside your head, 'I relax all the muscles in my feet.'

When you think of something, your body can respond to what you are thinking.

When you choose to think, 'I relax all the muscles in my feet,' your feet muscles can relax.

Notice any changes in the feelings in your feet muscles as they relax.

Notice if your feet become warm, tingly or cool.

Notice if your feet appear light in weight, or heavy in weight.

Whatever the feelings in your feet, as your feet relax, notice the feelings.

You may choose to think of some of your other muscles and relax those too.

You may choose to think, 'I relax all my leg muscles, all my back muscles, all my stomach muscles.'

Those muscles can then relax.

Then relax your neck muscles.

Then relax your shoulder muscles.

Then relax your jaw muscles.

Then go on like that, relaxing all the muscles in your body.

Or if you prefer, you may choose to think, 'I relax all the muscles in my body.'

If you choose, you can relax all your muscles at the same time. It is as simple as that.

Allow the relaxation to flow throughout your body.

Notice any changes in the feelings in your muscles as your body relaxes.

Allow the weight of your body to sink a little deeper into the chair, or into the floor.

If you wish to change your body position to be more comfortable at any stage, then you can do so.

Notice whether you have developed a strong and steady pattern of breathing.

If you have closed your eyes, that is good.

Your body is relaxing.

If you have not yet closed your eyes, now is a good time to close your eyes, if you choose to do so.

As you continue to relax you can continue to hear any routine sounds which may, or may not, take place inside or outside the room.

If you choose to, allow to come into your mind's eye a nice picture of some
    sort.
The picture may be any nice picture; any nice picture at all.
The picture may be indoors or outside.
The picture may be any nice picture you have in your memory.
The picture may be something nice from today or a few days ago.
Or perhaps your nice picture may be from a long time ago.
You may be able to see your picture clearly or not clearly.
Your picture may look hazy and a bit out of focus.
It doesn't matter if your picture is not too clear in your mind's eye.
Your picture may be a moving picture, like on TV, or it may be a still pic-
    ture like a photograph.
Your picture may be in colour or it may be in black and white.
There may be people in the picture or there may be no people.

Notice the nice feelings inside you that go with the nice picture.
Notice whereabouts in your body your nice feelings are located.
Perhaps your nice feelings may be located in your stomach or in your head.
Some people have their nice feelings all over their bodies.

Keep the nice picture in your mind's eye for a few moments longer.
Keep your nice feelings while you think of a nice phrase or saying.
Choose one nice phrase or saying to say inside your head.
Such as: 'Tomorrow is another day'; or 'Every cloud has a silver lining'; or
    'The sun will still shine tomorrow.'
Or choose a saying of your own.
Repeat for a few moments, your nice phrase or saying inside your head.
Notice the nice feelings inside you that go with the nice phrase or saying.
Notice whereabouts in your body your nice feelings are located.
Perhaps your nice feelings may be located in your stomach or in your head.
Some people have their nice feelings all over their bodies.

Staying relaxed with your eyes still closed.
In a moment I will tell you about a simple reminder of your nice
    thoughts and feelings which you can use to take with you after this
    session is over.

All you need is a simple reminder to prompt your nice thoughts and feelings after this session is over.

The reminder I suggest is simply to touch yourself on the wrist.

Touch yourself on the wrist now for practice.

That's good, good. That's it.

Now return your hand to where it was a moment ago.

After this session is over, touch yourself on the wrist two or three times a
day, every day ... until you need to no longer.

When you do that, over a period of time, you may feel better, stronger,
more relaxed.

After this session is over, touch yourself on the wrist two or three times a
day, every day until you need to no longer.

When you do that, over a period of time you may feel better, stronger,
more relaxed.

Use this quick, touch on the wrist relaxation when you need it, when
you're wide awake, at home or outdoors, when you are walking, travelling or doing anything you usually do.

You do not need to be seated or lying down.

You do not need to be in a quiet place.

The touch on the wrist can be a simple prompt which starts your relaxation.

Just stay as you are relaxing nicely for a few more moments.

Relaxing for a few more moments.

Relaxing for a few more moments.

Relaxing for a few more moments.

In a moment I am going to count out loud from one to ten.

When I say the number ten, keeping hold of your calm feelings, open your
eyes, be refreshed and feel alert as usual.

1-2-3-4-5-6-7-8-9-10.

Open your eyes.

You are now refreshed, fully alert and ready to do everything as usual.

You are now refreshed, fully alert and ready to do everything as usual.

End of Session

REFERENCES

Beck, A. T. (1961). A Systematic Investigation of Depression. *Comprehensive Psychiatry*, 2 (3), pp. 163–170.

Cannon, W. B. (1929). *Bodily Changes in Pain, Hunger, Fear and Rage*. Reprinted (1970). New York: McGrath.

Deci, E. and Ryan, R. (2000). The 'What' and 'Why' of Goal Pursuits: Human Needs and the Self Determination of Behaviour. *Psychological Inquiry*, 11 (4), pp. 227–268.

Ecclestone, K. and Hayes, D. (2009). *The Dangerous Rise of Therapeutic Education*. Oxon: Routledge.

Ellis, A. (1955). New Approaches to Psychotherapy Techniques, Brandon VT. *Journal of Clinical Psychology Monograph Supplement*, 11, pp. 208–251.

Health and Safety Executive. (2003). *Draft Management Standards on Work Related Stress: Pilot Project*. London: HSE. www.hse.gov.uk/stress/stresspilot/index.htm

Holmes, T. H. and Rahe, R. H. (1967). The Social Readjustment Rating Scale. *J Psychosom Res*, 11 (2), pp. 213–218.

Krusche, A., Cyhlarova, E., King, S. and Williams, J. M. G. (2012). Mindfulness Online: A Preliminary Evaluation of the Feasibility of a Web-based Mindfulness Course and the Impact on Stress. *BMJ Open*, 2012 (2), pp. e000803. doi:10.1136/bmjopen-2011-000803

Layard, R. and Dunn, J. (2009). *A Good Childhood: The Landmark Report for the Children's Society*. London: The Children's Society.

Lazarus, A. A. (1992). Multimodal Therapy: Technical Eclecticism with Minimal Integration. In J. C. Norcross and M. Goldfried (Eds.) *Handbook of Psychotherapy Integration*, pp. 231–263. London: Basic Books.

Maslow, A. (1954). reprinted 1970. *Motivation and Personality*. New York: Harper.

Meichenbaum, D. (1974). *Cognitive Behaviour Modification*. Morristown: General Learning Press.

Mental Health Foundation. (2010). *Mindfulness Report*. www.mentalhealth. org.uk/publications/be-mindful-report/

Mitchell, L. (1987). *Simple Relaxation; the Mitchell Method for Easing Tension*. Edinburgh: John Murray.

National Healthy Schools Programme. (2006). *Wired for Health (WfH) 2004*. updated, 2006, www.wiredforhealth.gov.uk

Open University. (1992). *Handling Stress: A Pack for Group Work*. Department of Community Education, Course P922G. Milton Keynes: The Open University.

Padesky, C. A. and Mooney, K. A. (1990).Presenting the Cognitive Model to Clients. *International Cognitive Therapy Newsletter*, 6, pp. 13–14.

Palmer, S. and Cooper, C. (2007). *How to Deal with Stress*. London: Kogan Page.

Peck, M. S. (1978). *The Road Less Travelled*. London: Arrow Books.

Peck, M. S. (1988). *The Different Drum*. London: Arrow Books.

Peterson, C. and Park, N. (2003). Positive Psychology as the Evenhanded Positive Psychologist Views It. *Psychological Enquiry*, 14, pp. 141–146.

Peterson, C., Park, N. and Seligman, M. E. P. (2005). Orientations to Happiness and Life Satisfaction: The Full Life versus the Empty Life. *Journal of Happiness Studies*, 6, pp. 25–41.

Primary Review. (2007). *Community Soundings, Regional Witness Sessions, Interim Reports (First Report)*. London: Esmee Fairbairn Foundation and University of Cambridge.

Richards, A., Rivers, I. and Akhurst, J. (2008). A Positive Psychology Approach to Tackling Bullying in Secondary Schools: A Comparative Evaluation. *Educational and Child Psychology*, 25 (2), pp. 72–81.

Seligman, M. E. P. (2000). Positive Psychology. In J. E. Gillham (Ed.) *The Science of Optimism and Hope*, pp. 415–430. London: Templeton Foundation Press.

Westbrook, D., Kennerley, H. and Kirk, J. (2007). *An Introduction to Cognitive Behaviour Therapy: skills and applications*. London: Sage.

DISCLAIMER

The author's doctorate is in educational psychology, not medicine, and the contents of this programme are educational, not medical. The programme is designed along the lines of stress management tuition or coaching sessions; it is not medical treatment.

The author and publisher offer this as part of any self-help programme undertaken. It is not intended to replace your support network with friends and family.

Do not use these materials as a substitute for face-to-face professional advice such as you would normally access, for example from your family doctor.

It is important to keep yourself safe when using relaxation techniques. The techniques offered in this programme must be used only when safe to do so. Do not use these relaxation techniques or listen to the audio-recorded relaxation scripts whilst driving or controlling a vehicle. Do not embark upon or continue in a relaxed state when to do so would distract you from, or be incompatible with, looking after yourself or other people for whom you may be responsible, such as a member of the family needing your attention.

The author and publisher are not responsible for any negative consequences of using the information or resources provided here or in related websites or published material. By accessing and using this information you find here and on linked sites, you acknowledge that you release the author and publisher from all liability and responsibility associated with your use and interpretation of this content.

You acknowledge that this information and materials may contain inaccuracies or errors and we expressly exclude liability for any such inaccuracies or errors to the fullest extent permitted by law.

Your use of any information from this material or programme is entirely at your own risk, for which we shall not be liable. It shall be your own responsibility to ensure that any related products, services or information which you might use, meet your specific requirements.

Neither we nor any third parties provide any warranty or guarantee regarding the use of these materials.

INDEX

Locators in **bold** refer to tables and those in *italics* to figures.